Of Animals and Angels

Of Animals and Angels

MARGUERITE ANTONIO

iUniverse, Inc.
Bloomington

Of Animals and Angels

iUniverse books may be ordered through booksellers or by contacting:

iUniverse
1663 Liberty Drive
Bloomington, IN 47403
www.iuniverse.com
1-800-Authors (1-800-288-4677)

ISBN: 978-1-4697-0956-7 (sc)
ISBN: 978-1-4697-0957-4 (e)

Printed in the United States of America

iUniverse rev. date: 01/10/2012

Dedication

This book is dedicated to my grandsons,
Daniel and Declan, with love.

You are two of my favourite angels.

FOREWORD

We humans have documented the benevolent assistance of angelic presence in our lives since the beginning of recorded history. These wonderful interactions with the angelic realms may present through another human being, an animal, or another animate species, or the interaction may come from an inanimate source. Whichever it is, these angelic interludes leave us feeling protected, loved, more cognizant of life around us, and sometimes wiser than before. What a blessing this is.

It is my belief that everyone, upon searching and allowing his or her mind and heart to accept this phenomenon, will have angel stories to share.

Although the short stories and the characters within the book *Of Animals and Angels* are fictitious, I have been deeply inspired by the angelic presence in my own life and the presence in the lives of others who have shared their angel stories with me.

Read and enjoy.

Contents

THE ANGEL AND THE TRAIN

I can still remember the last time I'd heard her tell the story. My daughters, age eleven and eight years, and I had gone to visit my grandmother at the Seniors Lodge where she now resided. Hers was a small, self-contained one-bedroom apartment with a tiny kitchen and small sitting room. The girls sat on a settee across from Grandmother's favorite rocking chair, and she bade me get a chair from the kitchen for myself. We'd just finished tea served in bone china cups and saucers, along with her favourite peppermint cookies.

My eldest could no longer contain her excitement. "So, Great-Grandma, tell us the story again, please," she pleaded. Grandmother smiled.

My grandmother was a tiny lady, not five feet tall, with an hourglass figure that she retained until her death at age 106. Her blue eyes sparkled behind silver wire-rimmed glasses, and she had scraped her steel-grey hair back into a bun that sat low on the back of her head. Despite her best efforts, tendrils of silver escaped to curl softly about her tiny face.

Grandmother loved to tell the story and would always address it to me, when I was present, even when my own daughters sat in awe as their great-grandmother told the story of the angel and the train.

"It was shortly before the end of the Second World War," she would begin. "You, your parents and sister, and I all lived on my small acreage outside the town of Yarrow in the lower mainland of BC. Your daddy worked for the government, trucking war supplies to the ports in Vancouver. Most of the men were involved in the war effort, so, like many women in our community, your mom and I went out to the local farms to help with the harvest. We picked berries and hops and helped gather corn. On nice days, you two little ones would come with us and we would make a grand picnic with the other women and their children. Your daddy made little baskets so you could help with the harvest too. Despite the war raging in Europe, we had a good life here in the valley."

My grandmother, I remember, had a way of seeing the best in every situation.

"My property lay on the far side of the town from the other families," she would go on to explain, "so at the end of the day, we would all walk down the road together, chatting about our day. Then your mom and I would split away from the others to take a shortcut along the interurban tracks to where they intersected with the road to my place.

"Now the interurban," she would remind us, "was the famous, and now historic, British Columbia Electric Railway, which operated in the lower Fraser Valley, bringing people and supplies to and from the great city of Vancouver. The BCER has many spurs. The one passing our area came from Vancouver, around Sumas Mountain, through Yarrow to Chilliwack, and back to the city. Unlike the noisy, rattling, smelly diesel trains we have now, the interurban was quiet and very fast."

"That evening," grandmother would go on to say, "that evening with weather muggy and threatening rain, we worked longer than usual to bring in as much of the crops as we could before the rains began. Though you children had napped on a blanket in the shade, your mom and I were tired and hot as we trudged along the track. You ran a little ahead to explore. You always were an inquisitive little one," she'd say as she smiled at me briefly; then her eyes would cloud with the memory of what happened next. Her voice strained, she went on with the story. "*Toot, toot* and there it was—the big black train, bearing down on us from behind at full speed. We grabbed your sister and jumped off the tracks into the shallow ditch beside them as the train whizzed by. 'My baby,' your mom cried and tried to run after you, but I held her back.

"Ach, mein Gott," Grandmother cried in her native German language as she dropped her head into her hands as if to ward off the memory. "All I could see were your little feet in their white shoes running up the track as we huddled in the ditch, praying. Then at the last second, your little feet seemed to lift up off the ground."

Having heard the story so often over the years, I have tried to separate what was told from what I could remember. I don't know what caught my attention to make me run ahead. I do remember a loud *toot, toot* and there was a big black monster with lots of teeth and one big shining eye and it was coming fast. Really fast. I couldn't see Mommy or Omah, but I think I heard Mommy yell for me. But the monster was coming faster and trying hard to get me. I was so scared, but I ran my hardest 'cause I knew that if I could get to where the track crossed the road to Omah's house, I would be okay. But my legs couldn't run faster and the monster was almost there. Then suddenly there was a man, and he lifted me up high in his arms and carried me against his chest, and I felt safe. I felt safe and warm and loved, like when my daddy held me close, but this man wasn't my daddy. He held me like this for a time and then set me down on the grass by the crossing. The train whizzed by, and I could hear a car engine rattling on the road beside me, and it made me hot and it smelled. I was scared again. Where was the man? Where had he gone? Then I saw Omah running up the tracks to me, and my sister and Mommy too. Omah crouched down beside me to check and see if I was okay and gave me a big hug. Then Mommy was there hollering at me and crying and cuddling me tight. My big sister was crying too and looking awful scared.

My grandmother continued the story. "A man was standing beside his car, looking grey and shaken. His wife sat inside, crying. They were in shock. After ascertaining the child was fine, the driver explained that they had heard the whistle and had come to a stop, and then noticed the child running up the track in front of the train. They were terrified for the child but knew they couldn't possibly reach her in time. The train, he said, was almost upon her when they saw someone—a man, the driver seemed to think. He was just there, in the blink of an eye. He snatched the child up in his arms, got to the crossing seconds before the train, set her down on the grassy verge beside the track, and was gone. Gone! Just like that. A miracle, the couple in the car said. They would never forget this day and neither would we.

Later that evening we told your daddy about what happened. He held you close, very close, as tears filled his eyes. 'Baby, do you know who that man was?' he asked.

"'God's angel,' you replied sleepily.

"After we put you children to bed, your mom and daddy and I talked for hours, laughing, crying, and thanking God for sending an angel to your rescue. And I thank Him still today for the miracle that occurred that day," my grandmother stated, her eyes shining with love and faith.

I thank God as well. I've met my guardian angel several times over the years and feel his presence with me always.

LUCKY DOG

Ari slouched in the rocking chair on the deck above the patio of their home. One work-worn hand held a mug of coffee, the other a cigarette. A frown creased his weathered face as his gaze travelled over the yard and garden. After his retirement five years earlier, he and his wife, Meg, had travelled some, and he'd enjoyed it. But one could only be away from home for so long, he'd maintained. He liked his own bed. Now he puttered around the yard while Meg kept busy with charity work and the healing work she did at the local spa. Yes, Ari thought as he viewed the yard, when they had moved out here after his retirement, he enjoyed the challenge of building the greenhouse for Meg, making the raised gardens at the back and side of the house, building the new arbor at the entrance to the patio, and landscaping along the driveway. Yes, the yard looked good, he thought as he took another drag on his cigarette, but what other project could he get working on next? Winter would soon be upon them, curtailing any outdoor activities. Oh, Meg had a long to-do list for him of things that needed attention within the home, but he liked outdoor work. She had even suggested he do some kind of volunteer work, but he had always been a working man, damn it, and this laying about was getting him down.

"Hey, Meg, could a guy get a fresh cup of coffee out here, huh?" he yelled through the screen door.

"Just a minute. I'm on the phone."

"Yadda, yadda, yadda," Ari grumbled under his breath, his fingers drumming the arm or the chair. A few moments later, Meg pushed her way through the screen door, juggling a tray with the pot of fresh coffee, a plate of cookies, and an extra mug. She set the tray on the table beside Ari and plopped down on the other rocking chair.

"You could get up, walk into the kitchen, and get your own coffee, you know," Meg pointed out.

"Yeah I suppose I could," he replied with a huge sigh. He refilled his coffee cup, lit another cigarette, and then slouched back into his chair.

"Ari, I've decided to go to that Reiki seminar in Edmonton in September. Why don't you come along and spend some time with the children? It's only for the weekend. Davy would love to see his grandpa again. It would be good to get away for a bit, don't you think?"Meg said as she leaned forward, watching him closely.

"Nah, you go ahead. I'll just stay here and get the place in shape for winter."

"Okay then. I'll be leaving on the sixth," Meg stated, leaning back in her chair.

"Fine."

They sat in silence for a moment

"Looks like Susan's truck coming up the drive," Meg commented as she rose to meet their friend.

"Ari, come see. Susan has something to show us," Meg called a few moments later. Ari ambled down the path to the drive to see the two women chatting in front of the truck. A scruffy mutt tied with a piece of rope stood quietly at Susan's side.

"Picked up another stray, did you, Susie girl?" Ari teased gruffly. He still hadn't quite forgiven her for the stray cat she had pawned off on them last summer.

"Well, actually," Susan began with a concerned glance at Meg, and then went on to explain that she had seen the dog along the highway between there and town several times. She had thought he may be a farm dog that had wandered away, but each time she had seen him, he had looked scruffier and hungrier and more lost. That morning she had used some of the eggs she had been delivering to lure him close. He had gobbled them up and jumped into the truck and sat there calm as could be. Ari eyed Susan with suspicion, and the dog moved away from the humans but stood quietly watching.

"I can't take him home with me, Ari," she pleaded. "You know Muffy is ill and needs a lot of care right now, and a new dog in the yard would disturb the chickens who are just beginning to lay eggs again. And anyway, this fella just needs a place to stay until we can find his owner."

"No. Not again," Ari bellowed. "I am just getting used to the damn cat; now you want me to take on this mangy mutt? No way!"

"We could tie him on the patio for a few days. He wouldn't be in the way," Meg placated.

Ari glared at the dog and then stalked away. Meg shrugged apologetically. Then Ari turned with a sigh.

"All right, but he's your problem, not mine, Meg. Mind, we keep him only over the weekend," Ari warned Susan, muttering unhappily as he stalked away.

"It will be okay, Susan," Meg said, patting the other woman's arm. They tied the dog near the table on the patio, and Susan brought an old blanket from the truck for the dog to lay on in the shade. Meg went into the house to get some water and a dish of the dried cat food for the dog. He did not move to the food or water until the women were seated on the deck. Then ate his fill and lay down, watching their every move.

"He is very wary but not noisy. Notice he hasn't barked or growled once," Susan commented.

"I'll come by tomorrow morning to clean him up a bit and take some pictures. We can make up posters and tack them up around the neighborhood to let the owner know where to find his dog. Oh, and I'll bring over some of Muffy's food, so don't go buying any."

That evening, as Ari sat on the deck, the dog moved to the bottom of the steps, watching the man.

"Don't say much, do you, mutt?" Ari commented. "Well that's good. But mind you don't get to comfortable here," he admonished.

"We should take him for a walk before bedtime," Meg suggested.

"Guess it wouldn't hurt." Ari untied the dog and they headed out down the alley behind the house.

"I'll take him if you like," Meg offered.

"It's okay. I've got him."

"He leads well and heels smartly. He must have had some training. Did Susan put this choker chain on him or was he wearing it when she found him?" Ari asked as they walked along.

"No, she said she found him that way. We'll check for tattoos or other identifying markings when we clean him up tomorrow," Meg replied.

The next day, Susan and Meg tethered the dog in the backyard, Susan chatting soothingly the whole time. The dog stood docilely as they scrubbed him down and combed through his matted hair. Susan checked him over carefully for injuries or infection. Ari watched morosely from his rocking chair on the deck, not offering help or comment.

"He looks to be a black Lab cross of some kind. What do you think, Ari?" Susan commented after they had tied him back on the deck and she and Meg had sat down to a cup of tea.

"Yes, appears so," Ari replied. "D'you find any identification on him?"

"No, nothing."

"How old do you think the mutt is—two, maybe three years?"

"He could be around that age. He seems okay but malnourished and thin. His fur is ratty and dull but should return to a sleek black with healthy food, exercise, and some tender loving care.

Thank you both for taking him in for the weekend. I will do what I can to find his owner. I will be back on Monday to pick him up, either way," Susan said as she rose to leave.

Meg continued to care for the dog, and she and Ari took him for daily walks. He was looking better already, they both had to agree, but so far they had not heard him bark or growl, not even when they met with other dogs while walking. They let everyone they met know he was a stray and they were looking for his owner.

Ari answered the phone on Monday when Susan called to tell them she had had no response to the posters or ad she had placed in the local paper.

"I will have to take him to the city pound as a stray," Susan said sadly. "When do you want me to pick him up?"

"No!" Ari cried. "We keep him."

"Are you sure?" Susan asked reluctantly. "A dog is a big responsibility, Ari."

"We keep him," Ari said adamantly.

"Okay. Thank you, Ari. I know you two will be good for him." *And he will be good for you*, she added silently, for she knew how concerned Meg had been that Ari might again sink into dark moods and depression as he had over the last winter.

"Okay, mutt," Ari said as he sat in the rocking chair. The dog sat at the bottom of the steps, watching intently. "Here's the deal, dog. We keep you, feed you, and get you in shape, but you remember you are very lucky to be here." Ari thought for a moment and then smiled down at the dog.

"That's what we will call you. Come here, Lucky." The dog leapt up the steps and sat down beside the man. Ari was gently stroking Lucky's fur when Meg came out with two mugs of coffee. She glanced at the dog and raised an eyebrow at Ari.

"We have got ourselves a pet, Meg. I'm calling him Lucky!" Ari exclaimed with a smile. Meg said nothing but smiled broadly as well.

Under the couple's loving care, Lucky grew strong and healthy. A trip to the local veterinarian confirmed Susan's assessment that Lucky was indeed a black Lab cross and about three years old. His fur was now a sleek black pelt with socks of brindle on each foreleg. Ari kept busy building a gate in the arbor and strengthening the fence around the patio so the dog could roam freely within. He enlisted the help of a neighbor, Dennis, who he had met while walking Lucky, to design and build a room for the dog under the deck so he would be sheltered in all kinds of weather. Another dog-loving neighbor showed Ari and Meg a tract of sandy beach along the river where the dogs could be let off leash to run free. Bob and Elsie, who were both retired as well, would bring their Standard Poodle over for a play-date with Lucky. The dogs romped on the patio while the adults shared coffee and gossip on the deck. Bob had even managed to talk Ari into going with him to volunteer at the local SPCA. Ari had found he truly enjoyed working with the animal.

Later that fall, after Meg had returned from the seminar in Edmonton, friends gathered on the deck for coffee on a warm fall afternoon.

"Meg, I'm sure glad you're home," Dennis commented with a teasing grin at Ari. "Ari seems so lost without you!"

"Nah, I wasn't lost," Ari retorted, his big hand rested gently on the dog's shoulder. "I had Lucky to take care of me, didn't I, big guy? But we are glad she's back, aren't we, we lucky dogs," he added, smiling at his wife

"*Arf*," Lucky seemed to agree, and everyone chuckled. Susan caught Meg's eye and grinned. Yes, that dog had been a lucky find, an angel in disguise—just what Ari had needed at the time.

ANGEL HUGS

I t had been a long, enjoyable, but tiring trip. My daughter and grandson had flown to Vancouver from the Yukon ten days earlier. My husband and I had met them at the big Vancouver Airport. Our five-year-old grandson, Andy, had been awed and a little frightened by the noise and bustle of the big city but had settled nicely once we got them to our home in the Lower Fraser Valley. We, now retired and no longer feeling the need for two vehicles, had sold our second vehicle, a minivan, to our daughter and her husband. James had been unable to make the trip but Sharon was confident she could drive the minivan back to the Yukon. As I watched her drive up the lane to our home, I remembered how excited our grandson, Andy, had been when Grandpa had let him help wash the minivan and check the fluids for the trip up the coast to Powell River, where they planned on camping with friends and family. When Sharon had called the night before, I realized she and Andy were all played out and ready to go home.

"Hi there. How was the trip?" I asked, giving Andy a hug. He squirmed out of my embrace and stood to the side, pouting.

"Oh, Mom," Sharon said as she rested her head on my shoulder briefly, "I think our little man has had enough holiday for this year. We are anxious to head home, aren't we, son?" Andy just stood there looking miserable, saying nothing.

"Well, come on in. It's cooler inside, and Grandma baked some nice chocolate chip cookies this morning, just for you," my husband told Andy.

Sharon barely touched her evening meal, and Andy sat miserable and whining. I was very concerned about Sharon knowing she faced a three- to four-day road trip back to White Horse. I suggested I put Andy in a cool bath and she take a walk and I would give her a relaxing Reiki treatment (see appendix 3).

"I'd love that, Mom. Its cooler now and I love walking amongst the tall trees behind your place. We don't see the trees growing this tall in the Yukon, you know."

"Well, you, James, and Andy will just have to move down here then, wont you?" I quipped.

"Nice try, Mom," she replied with a grin. "Andy, behave for Grandma and Grandpa. I'll be right back."

"I'll load the dishwasher while you run a nice cool bath for this tired little man," Arnie suggested.

"Not tired," Andy whimpered but took my hand willingly as we headed to the bathroom.

"I think I may be able to find a few toys that your cousin Billy left behind after his last visit," I told the boy as I filled the tub with tepid water.

"Okay."

Soon Andy was splashing around in our big soaker-tub, playing with a toy boat I had found, pretending to be on the ocean. By the time Arnie joined us, Andy, who was now his old cheerful self, began sharing tales of his adventures on the beach, on the ferries, and on Grampy Abies big boat. I left the two of them to go and prepare the guest room-come-healing room for the Reiki session.

Sharon returned shortly after and was rummaging through their bags to find a pair of pajamas for Andy.

"And the ferry boat was really big, Grandpa, and we had to squeeze the car in with lots of others. Lucky the doors of the van opened to the side or we couldn't have gotten out. And, Grandpa, Mommy didn't ding the car once with all those others all around us," I heard him say proudly as the bathroom door opened and Sharon entered.

"Okay, Tiger, let's get you out of the tub and into some nice cool pjs," Sharon suggested.

"What's that?" Andy inquired, pointing at the Reiki table in the centre of the room.

"Well, Andy, your mommy is going to lay down on the table and I am going to do something with her that will make her feel better. It's called Reiki and it will help her to relax."

"Okay, and whatcha doing now, Grandma?" he asked again as I proceeded to turn on the tape to play soft music and light a candle on the low table in the corner that I used as a meditation centre.

"She is making the room nicer so we can relax more," Sharon explained.

"Can I get up on the bed?"

"Sure, Here you go," I said, lifting him onto the Reiki table.

"Okay, now it's Mommy turn," he exclaimed after a moment, and I lifted him back to the ground.

"Andy, I want you to lay back on the pillow there on your bed. You may watch as I do the healing work but you mustn't make a fuss, talk, or touch Mommy, okay. It won't take long but I want you to be very quiet while I work with Mommy."

" OK, Grandma, I'll be good," he promised as he went to lay on the sofa bed. Sharon and I smiled at each other as she hopped up on the table and got comfortable. I'd Reiki'd my daughters many times while training, and later as well, so Sharon knew the procedure, but Andy had never seen me doing a Reiki treatment before this, and I could see he was very curious.

"Just relax, honey. Meditate if you like," I said quietly to Sharon as I began the treatment by calling in the loving spirit-guided life-force energy that is Reiki. Beginning at the Crown Chakra, I placed my hand over the major chakras of her body with the intent of relaxing and loosening the tightness in her. Her neck and shoulder area seemed especially congested, so I raked off the excess energy by bringing my hand across her chest then down the arm to the wrist and flexing her hand to help release the pent-up energy there. I'd worked one side and had moved to repeat the process on the other side when Andy approached the table. I motioned him to go back to the bed, but he just smiled and brought his little hand up to Sharon' s arm, mimicking the rake-off motions I had just completed. He didn't touch her, merely slid his little hand down from shoulder to wrist a few times, and then looked up at me. I smiled and nodded as I moved to continue the treatment. Andy moved to the other side of the bed and preformed the same movements on her other arm. Sharon was now deeply relaxed and mumbling faintly. Andy looked around and then went over to the candle on the low table in the corner, cupped his little hand over it, and closed his fist as though holding the light. He brought it back to his mother, again running his hand down her arm. I was amazed. He looked at me for confirmation, and at my nod of approval, he continued to do this for a while; then he stepped back as though satisfied and returned to the sofa bed. Sharon meanwhile was even more relaxed.

"Grandma Susie!" she exclaimed aloud, smiling as tears seeped out of her closed eyes.

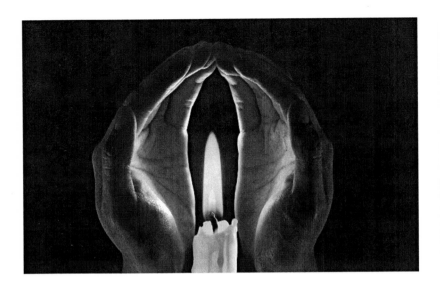

Andy rushed over, but I motioned him away and said it was okay as I finished the session and place them both in a protective circle of light. Sharon awoke slowly again, mumbling my deceased mother's name.

I was somewhat shaken by the power of this session and went out of the room to get us all a cool glass of water.

"But Great-Grandma Susie is dead, right?" Andy was saying as I reentered the room. Sharon had lifted him up onto the table, where she sat holding him.

"Yes, my mother, your great-grandmother, died before you were born, Andy. She is an angel in heaven now," I explained.

"Na, I saw her there," he pointed to the corner where the candle flicked. "She sended hugs to you, Mommy, and to you too, Grandma." He jumped from the table and dashed to the corner. "I'm gonna bring angel hugs to Grandpa too."

My daughter and I sat there in stunned silence as he again

cupped his hand over the candle and then carefully carried the light to my husband, who sat in the living room, reading.

"Oh. Mom, I saw her too. She was so beautiful, and her brown eyes shone so lovingly. I asked if she would like to meet Andy, and she glanced down at him with a big smile and then sort of faded away. Oh, Mom, it was awesome! What an experience! And Andy, well he just took it all in stride as though it was a normal occurrence. Wow!" Sharon was laughing and crying as we hugged one another.

"You certainly were in a deep, relaxed, and meditative state," I commented.

"But, Mom, Andy wasn't and he saw her too! He is the most awesome child."

"She must have chosen this moment to let you know all would be well and that you are both dearly loved. Grandma Susie would have been very proud of you, and of him too, Sharon."

"Wow. I feel so much better. We will be fine tomorrow and on the trip home."

"Yes, my dear. Yes, you will!" I replied, silently thanking the Reiki guides and my own guides and mentors as I put away the Reiki table and tidied the room.

Arnie came in, when I'd finished tidying the room, with the sleeping child cradled in his arms. He gently laid Andy on the bed. We stood quietly gazing at the sleeping child and I whispered a silent prayer thanking God for such innocence and for Andy's being able to recognize angels and convey their unconditional love.

MOMMA DUCKY

Henny and Drake cuddled on the end of the pier where the morning sun had already warmed the worn old boards. In front of them lay the placid waters of Hatzic Lake, with morning mist curling above it, veiling the distant mountains. Behind them, above a low knoll, the sun rose over the Great House, melting away the shadows along the pier inch by inch.

"Aha," Henny sighed. "Don't you just love this time of the morning? Everything is so fresh and still. This place is so beautiful and lush and friendly. I am going to hate to leave it."

Drake stirred, blinked twice, and reminded her again, "Don't get too comfortable, my dear. We will be joining the flocks heading south before the next full moon."

"Can't we stay, huh, Drake, just for this winter? Our little ones could use the extra time to grow and prepare, and anyway, others stay. Why, White Goose hasn't flown out for years and survives quite well. Besides, My Lady will take care of us."

"Henny, my dear, we have been over this before. It's time to go. That's the way it is. Now don't argue. Let me sleep for a few more moments before we wake the brood."

Henny moved a few inches away from Drake. He just didn't seem to understand, she thought. She and Drake had been together for over a year now and she loved him dearly, was comfortable in his love for her and their family, but sometimes he was so stubborn!

They had flown north with the flock to settled here on this beautiful lake, build their first nest together, and start their family. They had been so excited, exploring the shore and finger of land that jutted into the lake, before choosing their nesting site. She had chosen a spot beneath a large shrub across from the office of the Great House, above the spot where she and Drake now sat. Drake had been hesitant about that site at first, but to Henny it seemed right. Drake, she had realized, had had little contact with humans and civilization before their getting together, but Henny's flock had settled on an inhabited river bank when she was younger, so she had less fear of humankind and civilization than he. So after a little more exploring and his getting to be more comfortable with the place, they had settled on her chosen site.

Henny turned now to gaze fondly at their first nesting site. She remembered her first meeting with My Lady and chuckled softly. Drake had been off somewhere doing whatever males do. She and a few others had wandered into the gardens at what she had later thought of as the Great House. The humans there had hosted a party around the fire pit the night before and left a few tasty tidbits around the grounds for her and her friends to enjoy.

They had been fluttering about, squawking and feasting on the bounty, when a door slammed and the lady appeared.

"Ah, what have we here? Jake, come take a look," she called back into the house. At the sound of her voice, Henny's friends raced away, half flying, half running, quacking loudly. My Lady stood there laughing as the man came out to see what all the racket was about. Henny, however, hadn't run away. She waited for a moment, assessing the lady's mood before moving closer.

"Look, Jake, this one isn't afraid. I think she is the one who has been setting up a nest under the Rhody in front of the office. Remember I told you about them, how they were so carefully building a snug nest. Bring me some of that grain I bought, Jake. I'll stay here and talk to her. Come here, little one," she crooned, crouching down on her haunches and holding out a hand. Henny had watched, curious but not really afraid of this lady. She seemed to have an aura of calm and love about her that attracted not just herself but a good number of other life forms on this side of the lake. White Goose adored this human, whom many called My Lady. The man brought out a packet and the lady opened it, placing a small amount of grains in the palm of her hand, extending it out toward Henny. Timid but curious, Henny moved closer then quickly grabbed a few kernels and jumped back. The lady kept talking softly, her voice lulling Henny's fears. Henny moved closer again, and as she snacked on the grains, the lady ran the back of her forefinger gently over Henny's head. What a sensation that had been! So loving and gentle. Drake, Henny remembered now, had been annoyed with her for getting so close to a human.

The next time they had encountered My Lady, Drake watched from a distance as Henny approached to sit beside the lady on the pier. He had said nothing at the time but later commented that he could understand why everyone in the area loved her.

Beside Henny, Drake stirred and ruffled his feathers, watching her intently. "Doing a bit of reminiscing, are you, my dear?" he said softly, drawing nearer to her.

"Yes, I was remembering how I first met her, My Lady," she answered.

"I will not forget how she saved our first nest from that awful dog."

"Oh," Henny shuddered, "don't remind me. We wouldn't have our little family but for her."

"That is true."

He had not been so frightened in all his life before. Henny had laid ten perfect eggs and was sitting on them day and night, protecting and incubating them lovingly. He had ventured out to gather food for her when, at a distance, he'd heard her frantic quacking. He had flown back to the nest as quickly as he could, but by then, My Lady had shooed away a big dog that had been pestering Henny, trying to invade their nest. It took some time to calm Henny and straighten the nest, but none of the eggs had been harmed, thanks to My Lady's intervention. Later that evening, the lady had brought the man along and they had built a sturdy fence around the shrub under which the nest sat and had even provided a dish for water and one for grains for Henny. Each day after that, My Lady had replenished the water and small dish of grain for them within the protected shelter of the fence. Drake still foraged for the nutritious seaweeds and wild seed for Henny but felt much more at ease when he had to leave her in the nest.

"Yes, and I remember the other dog incident," Henny chortled. "Now that's a fine tale to tell our children's children one day."

"That is a story best forgotten," he retorted, but she could see the flash of amusement in his eye.

It had happened on this very pier. Henny and the brood had been sunning on the warm boards while Drake was away with some of the males, scouting the fields to the south. Scampy, always the curious one, had waddled farther along the shore toward the neighbouring property. Henny, half-dozing, hadn't been paying close attention until she heard a furious barking and Scampy squawking. She was half flying, half running back into the water to get back to the pier with Brutus, the neighbour's big dog, snapping at her tail. Henny hissed for the others to get into the water and race to the reeds around the bend where she and Drake had secured a snug, protected nest, even as she flew to the lake to place herself between the dog and Scampy. White Goose, a friend of the family, was, despite having a permanently injured wing and one blind eye, fluttering about, screeching and whistling, trying to distract Brutus. Henny had managed to slip between Scampy and the dog. She flapped her wings and sqawked loudly, trying to distract him, while rushing the rest of the brood away. But Brutus was determined. He was not to be denied what he thought to be a tasty tidbit.

My Lady rushed out of the office to see what was happening.

"No, Brutus, no. Come back here!" she yelled. The dog paid her no heed.

"Fred, get that dog out of the water!" My Lady screamed at her neighbour, who was, by now, out on his deck.

"Brutus, come," he whistled for the dog, who, again, paid no attention. "Drat you, you big mutt, come here!" Fred dove into the lake with a mighty splash and swam powerfully, calling his dog.

It really must have been a comical sight to behold, Henny

mused in retrospect, though at the time it was anything but funny. There were the young ones paddling furiously to get away, herself one minute urging them forward, the next turning on the swiftly approaching dog, and White Goose fluttering, honking, and whistling loudly. Brutus was barking and snapping at Henny, and Fred was swimming strongly as he yelled for the dog to come back. Drake flew into this tableau with a mighty screech and landed on Fred's back, quacking and pecking at the man's head. It was Fred's roar as he splashed about, trying to unseat Drake, that eventually caught the dog's attention. When Drake finally realized it was the dog not the man that had posed the threat to his family, he gracefully lifted off the man and flew to where Henny and the brood were rounding the bend to safety.

Henny caught Drake's frown as she chuckled with the memory.

"That was not funny! And we will not be discussing that incident again," he hissed, but she saw humour lurking in his eye as shadow fell across the area where they sat. Henny turned to look.

"Ah, it's My Lady's daughter, Drake. You know, the one who came to visit with her wee one," Henny exclaimed.

Drake glanced over his shoulder. "So it is. Maybe she is in the habit of doing her morning meditation here like My Lady does. If so, she won't bother us." He ruffled his feathers and then settled down again.

A few moments later, Henny nudged Drake. "She is looking very sad, not relaxed at all, Drake. I wonder what's the matter. I am going to get closer and try to cheer her up a bit."

"Leave her be, Henny. Not all humans appreciate the wild life intruding, you know."

"I won't disturb her," Henny said as she quietly waddled closer to My Lady's daughter. The young woman sat still, gazing out onto the lake, tears rolling quietly down her soft cheek.

"*Quack, quack*," Henny spoke softly as she stood in front of her. The young woman started but then smiled slightly. "Ah, you must be mom's momma duck. Are you the one?" A shadow passed over them again as My Lady came out with two mugs of steaming coffee and sat down beside the younger woman. The daughter gratefully took the mug and buried her face in the warm steam, trying to hide her tears.

"I see you have met my friend," My Lady said as Henny waddled closer. She reached into her pocket for a few grains, placing them in her palm. Henny waddled closer still and reached into My Lady's palm for the kernels as the lady gently ran her knuckle of her forefinger over the duck's head.

"She is quite tame, you see. That's her mate lounging at the end of the pier. Her nest, with all ten of the ducklings, is over around the bend."

Henny gave a sharp quack, Drake whistled, and the ducklings came scurrying out of the reeds to where their parents sat. Some flew low over the water, others swam quickly, their feet paddling so fast they were a mere blur in the water. One, flapping her wings and paddling at the same time, landed beside her mother in front of the two women, sliding on the warm boards, nearly landing back in the water again.

"That would be Scampy. Remember, honey, I told you about the ducks, the dog, and the man," My Lady said with a chuckle as she reached into her pocket for more seeds and threw them along the boards. My Lady wrapped her arm around her daughter's waist as they sat watching the antics of the ducklings as they scrabbled for the food.

"Ah, Mom, it's so beautiful here. I hate to leave," she said sadly, "but I miss Erik and our life in the Yukon as well. I feel so torn and a little afraid too. Thoughts of a new baby and being so far away from family are a bit daunting at times."

"We've loved having you and little Davy here with us these last weeks, dear. My, how he has grown, even in this last little while. Erik won't know his boy anymore."

"Yes, hasn't he grown. He's such a good baby," she said as she turned to face her mother. "And I have really appreciated all your help and good advice. It's not always easy being a new mom, but I feel a lot more confident now. Thank you. I love you, Mom."

"I love you too, dear, very much," My Lady said, hugging her daughter close, and she added, "You will find that that's a mother's roll: teaching, I mean. Look at momma duck here with her brood of ten. They were hatched only this spring and are now almost ready to fly away. Quite a feat, wouldn't you say?"

The younger woman chuckled. "I fly north and they fly south, and here you are in the middle."

"Yes, that's right. We'll be sad to see both you and Davy, and this little family leave, but, honey, that is the way it is in life. You and Erik have a good life in the Yukon, though," she added with a twinkle in her eye. "I'm sure you could find a good one here as well."

"Nice try, Mom," the younger woman answered with a laugh. "Maybe one day we will wander back south, but not yet, I think. However, it sure is good to visit." The two women sat in comfortable silence for a moment.

"Mom, when momma ducky and her brood go south, do they return here next year?"

"Sometimes the parents do, but the ducklings will most likely have struck out on their own by then. That's the way life is. Now, how about I make breakfast while you check on your little man?" My Lady suggested as she rose. The ducklings scattered back into the water and swam toward the middle of the lake. Henny moved over by Drake, settling close as she kept an eye on the brood.

"So, when do we meet with the rest of the flock heading out?" she asked with a sigh.

Drake watched her closely. "You ready to leave now? We can meet with the group in the fields over the next rise later today if you like."

"Yes, I'm ready to leave now. That's the way it is in life."

"And thank you, My Lady, for helping me to see, for being our guardian angel and guiding light," Henny murmured quietly as she gazed at the big house for a moment before she and Drake flew away.

AN ANGEL AT THE SCENE

"Joan," Rob called to his wife, who sat chatting with their daughter, Elsie, at the kitchen table, "come see what I found." After folding the paper to show her the advertisement, he handed it to his wife and sat back watching as she read the ad.

"Mmm, it looks like the car you've been searching for," she commented as she laid the paper down beside him and went back into the kitchen.

Later that evening, Rob broached the subject again, asking George, his son-in-law, how to get from their home to the dealership where the 1987 Lincoln Town Car was advertized for sale. George, after seeing the ad and chatting with Rob about the pros and cons of such a purchase, suggested he and Rob drive over to the dealership in the morning. Joan hadn't paid a lot of attention as the men made these plans. She knew Rob wasn't happy driving or riding in her smaller vehicle and had complained about it on the trip from Vancouver to Calgary. Rob had always driven, and felt more comfortable in, bigger cars or his service truck. However, when he had sold his business, and the service truck with it, they had agreed to economize and make do with her smaller car. That didn't stop Rob from dreaming about owning a big boat again.

"Wow, hon, you'll love this beauty," Rob rhapsodized when the men returned from checking out the car. "One owner, mint condition, low mileage on the odometer. It really is a good buy." Joan knew she could trust Rob and George to make a knowledgeable decision about vehicles as both were older car buffs and mechanics as well. But, personally, she found those bigger cars to be a greater challenge to drive. However, she agreed to go take a look at it later that day.

The Lincoln Town Car did look nice, with its gleaming white exterior and blue leather seats. The motor purred quietly and the car rode over the bumps in the road gentle as a feather. Joan had to admit she was impressed, so they bought the car on condition the dealer touch up the paint on the left fender where it was slightly scraped. Also, Rob wanted new tires on the front wheels and an alignment done, so the salesperson agreed to have the car ready for pickup the following afternoon.

"This calls for a celebration," Rob said happily as they drove back to their daughter's home. "Why don't we take the kids out for dinner tonight. I think they would enjoy a meal out at the Olive Garden or the Old Spaghetti Factory, don't you?"

"Yes, I think they would enjoy that," Joan replied. "You really are happy with this vehicle, aren't you, Rob? I didn't realize how much owning a Lincoln meant to you."

"I just don't feel as safe in these little beaters, I guess," Rob replied, referring to her Toyota, as they rolled up to the light to make a left turn onto the street that would take them to Elsie's place. The light turned green, and as the street ahead was clear of traffic, he followed a row of other cars making the left turn. As they entered the intersection, Joan spotted a gravel truck coming around the bend ahead. She touched Rob's arm. "There's a truck coming," she cried. Rob glanced to his right.

"Lots of time," he said as he continued through the intersection. However, the cars ahead had slowed and the truck was coming very fast.

"Rob, move it!" Joan screamed, but there was no place to go. Everything seemed to happen in slow motion. Through the windshield of the fast-moving truck, Joan saw the older truck driver's grimace as he applied the brakes. Tires squealed, and she was sure she could smell the burning rubber, but the truck kept coming. She saw only the front of the truck and then only the grill. Panicking, Joan tried to undo her seat belt so she could perhaps move to straddle the console between the front seats. She glanced at Rob, who bent forward and gripped the steering wheel with white knuckles, trying to inch forward as much as the space in front of him would allow. Then it came: a loud, crashing *bang* and the scream of tearing metal. All the air seemed to be drawn out of the car. Then nothing.

"I can't breathe." was her first panicky thought when she became aware again. Joan hadn't thought she had said it out loud until a gentle voice beside her told her to lean back, close her eyes, and take slow, shallow breaths. She did and it hurt, but small whiffs of air did get into her starved lungs.

A hand touched her right arm.

"Don't move, ma'am, and keep your eyes closed until I can brush the glass from your hair and face, okay," a younger woman's voice commanded. Joan still felt the gentle presence at her left but couldn't seem to move her head to see who it was.

"Open your eyes and look at me now," the women by her window said urgently. Joan tried to comply but couldn't seem to move about at all. The women put fingers to Joan's neck and leaned into the car to shine a light into her eyes. Joan's eyelids snapped shut but she forced them open again on command. "Where do you hurt?" the woman's voice asked.

"Can't breathe. Hurts," Joan whispered. The person, a paramedic, Joan realized, ducked back out of the window, and Joan heard snatches of conversation about needing a cervical collar, jaws of life, cutting the car away from around her.

Rob, where was Rob? Joan's mind scrabbled about, trying to remember, as she slowly turned her head to the driver's side of the car. A gentle hand touched her left arm.

"It's okay, my dear, your husband is shook up a bit but fine. Look out the front window. He is being seen to by the paramedics. He is okay. Just keep breathing slow and easy. You are going to be fine. I will stay with you as long as it takes. I promise."

Breathing slowly as instructed, trying to ignore the pain, Joan glanced out the shattered front windshield. Rob was out there, walking around. The car was facing the opposite direction to which they had been travelling. The gravel truck stood motionless up ahead, its driver talking to a policeman. The truck must have hit the car just behind the passenger seat. Her side of the door was buckled inward, crushing her to the console and the roof, she realized, pushing down on her head. Ow, but she hurt! She could move her legs though, at least a little, so that was good, right?

"Very good, my dear," the gentle voice beside her applauded. "You are doing fine. Just let the paramedics do their thing." Joan tried to see him but the light on her left was so bright he seemed to be part of it, or appeared as merely a shadow within it.

The paramedic was back, telling Joan that she and her partner were going to place a collar snugly around her neck, try to get her vitals, and access her condition, and then they would place a tarp over her so they could cut the remnant of the car from around her. Joan remained as still as she could as they moved her this way and that, gently, to accomplish what was needed. She tried not to cry out or moan but oh, how it hurt!

"That's good, ma'am. We will give you something for the pain once you are in the ambulance and we can start an IV. You are doing great. Now, it's going to be dark under the tarp and noisy as they cut the metal around you. They have done this many times before so don't worry, okay? It will take only a few more minutes and we will have you safely in the ambulance."

"My, husband?" Joan croaked.

"He is fine. We will take him with us to the hospital for further checkup just to be sure, though he seems fine. Don't worry, ma'am. Just stay calm and we will see to him and you," the young paramedic told her.

It was very dark and warm beneath the tarp. Joan tried to relax and allow things to follow their course. The pain was no better, but her breathing, she thought, was a little easier. She realized that the man was still with her, sitting in the driver's seat. He asked questions about her family and life in soft, soothing tones. They chatted but she would not, later, remember what about. It did serve to distract her, though, from the dark, the heat, and the pain.

After what seemed like hours, the tarp was removed and two strong paramedics bent to lift her from the wreckage and onto the stretcher. She tried to turn and thank the man who had stayed with her but the pain was so sharp when they moved her that all went black again.

Later, in the ambulance, Joan woke to see Rob sitting across from her behind the young paramedic who was attending her.

"Ah, you are awake again. Good, I have a few questions and then I'll administer something for pain," the young woman said. "Your husband gave me some particulars. You have some allergies to medications, I believe?" Joan answered as best she could though her throat hurt and her mouth was dry. The paramedic had put an intravenous line into her arm, Joan noticed, so after asking a few more question, an analgesic was administered through the IV. By the time they reached the emergency room at the local hospital, she was in much less pain and able to breathe more easily. The emergency room seemed very busy, but shortly after they arrived, an orderly took both Joan and Rob for X-rays and then back to a cubicle where Joan was given a bed while they awaited a doctor.

"Oh, my but this was your lucky day," the doctor exclaimed after he introduced himself to Rob and Joan. "You, sir, came out of that wreck with only minor scratches but may have a sore chest and shoulder where the seat belt dug in. Luckily, the car you were driving was equipped with them and with safety glass. The glass shatters, leaving a lot of mess but doing little damage, thank God. You, madam," he turned to Joan with a smile, "may be sore for a few days. You've several cracked ribs and a large contusion on your right elbow. Put ice on the elbow when you get home and take care not to strain your ribcage. I'll give you a prescription for pain medication. That and rest are the best medicine. We will let you go home, but if there are any other symptoms or the pain becomes worse, please come back. Now, I hear your car was towed away. Is there someone we can call to pick you up?"

Rob explained that they were visitors and gave him Elsie's phone number. When the doctor returned to let them know Elsie had been contacted and was on her way, Joan thanked him and asked if the others who had attended the scene of the accident were present, as she wanted to thank them too.

"We would like to thank you for your prompt attention at the scene of the accident," Rob told the young paramedic when she came by the cubical where they sat.

"And I really appreciate that man staying with me in the car for the whole time I was trapped," Joan added.

The paramedic looked puzzled. "I heard there were two off-duty policemen parked across the road waiting for the light to change. Apparently they witnessed the whole thing and called it in immediately. That's why we were able to respond so quickly. I believe one helped you out of the car," she said, turning to Rob, "and did a quick evaluation of your condition while the other one directed traffic around the accident."

"He, or someone, was in the driver-side seat with me almost the whole time. Didn't you see him there?" Joan asked. "I'd like to know who it was so I can thank him too."

"Well, I don't know, ma'am. But I do know you two are very lucky to be alive. Just this morning there was another accident with a gravel truck at the same stoplight. Two of the people in that car did not survive. Your guardian angels must have been with you today. That's all I can say!" she said with a smile and left.

Later that evening as they settled by the fireplace talking about what had happened, Joan asked Rob if he had seen where the policeman who had helped him out of the wreckage had gone.

"I don't know, my dear," he answered as he touched her hand gently. "Things were happening so fast, I just don't remember."

"But he, or someone, crawled back into the car and stayed with me there until the paramedics cut an opening and pulled me out. I'm not sure I could have made it without his calming words," Joan said with a quiver in her voice.

"Maybe he was your guardian angel, like the paramedic said," Elsie whispered as she leaned in to hug both her parents.

"Maybe he was. Yes, maybe he was." Joan tried to visualize the man again in her mind's eye.

"Thank you!" Joan whispered on a sigh.

THE THERAPIST IS A DOG

R ecently, I had the privilege of following along with Sandi as he made his rounds at the hospice and critical care unit of the local hospital. And what an honour that was! Everywhere he went, Sandi elicited cuddles and smiles from both the staff and the patients. It may have been the enthusiastic bounce in his step as he made his way down the corridors, the unconditional love shining in those deep brown eyes, or the mass of fluffy white-blond fur that lightened the mood in what was often a sterile, tense, and harried atmosphere. Whatever it takes to bring a few moments of joy into this setting, Sandi certainly has it. Sandi is a Standard Poodle and Golden Retriever cross. He is a Registered Therapy Dog.

Several organizations across Canada provide the opportunity for volunteers and their animals to visit patients in institutional settings. They visit hospitals, hospices, and nursing homes, as well as children's hospitals and seniors care centres, bringing their own unique brand of loving care to the patients there. Sandi and his handler, Sue, are registered volunteers with the St. John Ambulance Therapy Dog Service. This program began in Petersburg, Ontario, in 1992, and quickly spread across Canada. There are now over 450 volunteers in this service here in British Columbia, and about 115 of them do visitations in the Lower Mainland. Although they do not train the dogs themselves, the St. John Ambulance Service Therapy Dog Program has strict rules by which the dog and handler must adhere.

Sandi is still a pup (just over two years old) but has learned to be obedient and calm at all times. He is able to handle crowds and elevators and give way to and not be afraid of hospital equipment, like wheelchairs and gurneys. He is unfazed by the shuffling of slippers or the flapping of hospital gowns. Sandi is gentle and friendly to all and senses, very quickly, those who would prefer not to be approached by a dog, and he respects their space. Sue had to pass certain requirements as well, attend a training program, and commit to taking Sandi to the hospice and hospital on a weekly basis. The continuity of visitation by the same dog at the same time every week gives staff and patients alike something to look forward to. Medical professionals have acknowledged that stroking and petting a dog can calm patients, reduce blood pressure, and ease tension. I certainly witnessed his gentle calming effect as I followed Sandi on his rounds that day.

Sue and Sandi have been visiting the hospice and acute care areas of our local hospital one day per week for a year now. Their first stop, after dropping off our coats in the staff room, was always the hospice floor. Here the nurses greeted Sandi like an treasured friend. Several, knowing he would be there that day, carried doggy treats in their pockets for him. Sandi knew most of the patients and was greeted with warm hugs and cuddles. He is amazingly gentle for a big dog.

One patient, who lay in an elevated bed, called to Sandi as we entered his room. Sandi bounded over, raised himself up with his paws on the bed, and licked the man's face until he chuckled in delight.

In another area, two sisters sat with their dying father in a room rife with sadness and despair. Sandi ambled into the room, went straight to the bed, and touched his nose to the man's hand briefly. Then he moved first to one sister and then the other, placing his head in their laps, inviting strokes and cuddles. Of course they complied, and the somber aura of the room lifted noticeably. Later, as Sue and I chatted quietly with the sisters, Sandi flopped down on the floor and stretched out in a totally relaxed state that, in itself, was calming to behold.

One patient said she didn't much care for dogs but her husband, who was visiting at the time, had already motioned for Sandi to come into the room. As the man and the dog tussled playfully, the patient giggled at their antics, her tired eyes sparkling for just a few moments. Her husband mouthed his thanks as we left, his eyes shining with gratitude.

Reaching the acute care area a while later, we came upon a flurry of activity as a new patient was being admitted. We respectfully moved out of the way with Sandi. A young girl stood tearfully beside the gurney of the new patient. Then she spied Sandi.

"Oh. What a beautiful dog. May I pet him?" At Sue's nodded consent, the girl approached Sandi, touching the back of her hand to his nose. Sandi sat back on his haunches, leaning into the girl. She crouched down to hug him and bury her face into his soft fur, weeping softly.

"Honey, they are taking Grandma to her room, now," the girl's mother called softly as she approached. The young girl gave Sandi one last hug and stood calmly to follow her mother. Later, the mother caught up with us.

"My daughter was so upset to see my mother collapse earlier today and just didn't know how to handle things, first the paramedics rushing in and then the hurried trip to the hospital following the ambulance. Having the dog here did wonders for her. Thank you so much," she said as she clasped Sue's hand warmly and bent to pet Sandi.

Except for a break where he stopped to lap a bowl of water and we took him outside for a few moments, Sandi was on duty for a full two hours. I found it a bit tiring and certainly emotionally draining following him on his rounds, yet Sandi seemed to love it. He gave unconditionally to all who wanted and needed his special brand of loving care. I commented on this as I expressed my admiration of Sandi and his work, and of Sue and her commitment to it.

"Sandi is a very calm and loving animal. How could I not share him?" was her reply.

"Does this affect him in any way?" I asked.

"No. He loves it," she replied. "But when the two hours are up and I take him outside, he will often roll and roll around on the hospital lawn. It's as if he needs to rid himself of all the heaviness, sadness, and negativity collected while in there. But in a week he is excited and ready to be back here again."

Our last stop was the administrator's office. Sue let Sandi off leash, and he bounded quietly down the carpeted corridor to her office. The administrator handed him a doggy cookie and ruffled his fur gently after he sat before her quietly at her command.

"Ah, but you are quite the communicator, aren't you, Sandi?" she said with a grin as she fed him another treat. *She has that right,* I thought. Sandi does communicate an unconditional love and joy that warms the heart. What wonderful therapy that is.

APPENDIX

For Your Information

1. The British Columbia Electric Railway mentioned in the story "The Angel and the Train" did indeed exist. By the mid-nineteenth century, electricity had come into use in Europe and Asia as fuel for trains, as well as to replace gaslights on city streets (in 1883, the first electric street lighting system was switched on in Victoria, BC). The British Columbia Electric Railway Company was formed in April of 1897. Rails were laid and power stations secured, expanding the electric rail system in the Greater Vancouver area and Vancouver Island. In the year 1910, the BCE Fraser Valley interurban line to Chilliwack opened. The last passenger run on that line was on September 30, 1950, and the last interurban line

closed in 1958. These electric trains, which could reach a speed of 80 mph, had opened up the farming communities along the Fraser Valley. They were quieter and much more environmentally friendly than the diesel and diesel-electric trains of today.

There has been a concerted effort by the Fraser Valley Heritage Society to lobby the government of British Columbia to reinstate the interurban in the Fraser Valley. Thus far, discussions on this subject have not reached any definitive conclusion.

References include: www.trainweb.org,
Watts, David A. *All Time List of Canadian Transit Systems.*

2. Sandi of the story "The Therapist is a Dog" is an exceptional animal, and there are many others like him who bring a calming sense of peace to those who pet and cuddle them. As mentioned in the story, the St. John Ambulance Therapy Dog Service has been in existence in Canada since 1992. Their website offers information about how to become a volunteer as well as where to request their services: www.sja.ca.

My sincere thanks to Sandy Forward and her dog, Murphy, for sharing their time and allowing me to take pictures of him with me. It was their work, commitment, and dedication that inspired this story. It is the pictures of Murphy at work that are included in this story.

Dogs and other animals have also been used to assist the blind (www.cnibc.com). Animals be trained to assist people with a variety of hidden disabilities, such as seizures, life-threatening medical problems, mental disorders, and chronic pain. These animals seem to sense impending danger, can help the patient to function more efficiently, can help prevent injuries, and can even call for help in a crisis. The Canadian Foundation for Animal-Assisted Support Services, www.cf4aass.org, offers a wealth of information about these marvelous four-legged friends—angels all.

3. Reiki, as mentioned in the story "Angel Hugs," is spirit-guided life-force energy that can be used, sent, or transferred during a Reiki treatment. These treatments are deeply relaxing, promoting relaxation on the mental, physical, emotional, and spiritual level. Reiki energy helps to balance the body systems, encourages the release of disease, and enhances the body's own healing mechanism. Reiki is an ancient healing art/technique that dates back to times before Christ. Anyone can learn to do these techniques and practice the healing art on themselves or others.

    My book, *Reiki: An Ancient Healing Art Revisited,* is available through my website, www.reikirevisited.com, and at www .iuniverse.com.

CPSIA information can be obtained at www.ICGtesting.com
Printed in the USA
LVOW080340030212

266796LV00001B/3/P

9 781469 709567